I0413518

NISTIR 7681

A Semantic Product Modeling Framework and Language for Behavior Evaluation

Jae Hyun Lee
Steven J. Fenves
Conrad Bock
Hyo Won Suh
Sudarsan Rachuri
Xenia Fiorentini
Ram Sriram

National Institute of
Standards and Technology
U.S. Department of Commerce

NISTIR 7681

A Semantic Product Modeling Framework and Language for Behavior Evaluation

Jae Hyun Lee
Steven J. Fenves
Conrad Bock
Hyo Won Suh
Sudarsan Rachuri
Xenia Fiorentini
Ram Sriram
Manufacturing Systems Integration Division
Manufacturing Engineering Laboratory

April 2009

U.S. Department of Commerce
Gary Locke, Secretary

National Institute of Standards and Technology
Patrick D. Gallagher, Director

A Semantic Product Modeling Framework and Language for Behavior Evaluation

Jae Hyun Lee, Steven J. Fenves, Conrad Bock, Hyo Won Suh, Sudarsan Rachuri, Xenia Fiorentini, and Ram Sriram

Design Process Group
Manufacturing Systems Integration Division
Manufacturing Engineering Laboratory
National Institute of Standards and Technology
Gaithersburg, MD 20899
March 2010

Abstract

Supporting different stakeholder viewpoints across the product's entire lifecycle requires semantic richness for representing product related information. This paper proposes a multi-layered product modeling framework that enables stakeholders to define their product-specific models and relate them to physical or simulated instances. The framework is defined within the Model-driven Architecture and adapted to the multi-layer approach of the architecture. The data layer represents real world products, the model layer includes models of those products, and the meta-model layer (M2) defines the product modeling language. The semantic-based product modeling language described in this paper is specialized from a web ontology language enabling product designers to express the semantics of their product models explicitly and logically in an engineering-friendly way. The interactions between these three layers are described to illustrate how each layer in the framework is used in a product engineering context. A product example is provided for further understanding of the framework.

Keywords: Multi-layered product modeling framework, ontological product modeling, model-driven architecture.

1. Introduction

Efficient collaboration is essential when products are designed by temporally and spatially separated engineers. Collaborative environments enable product designers to interact and reach agreement by sharing design knowledge and product information [Sriram 2002] [Szykman 2001a] [Szykman 2001b]. Ontology can play a role in the environments as a shared product information model because ontology is a formal and explicit specification of a shared conceptualization [Gruber 1995]. The collaboration environment needs the support of a generic product modeling language that: (1) can be readily specialized for the products at hand; (2) can provide information to all stakeholders throughout the product lifecycle; and (3) provides explicit, logical semantics of the concepts and relationships involved without requiring that the stakeholders be versed in ontological thinking.

Ontological multi-layered product modeling frameworks provide the above capabilities [Bock 2009]. Figure 1 shows a high level view of our framework. Engineers can describe their product-specific models using a given semantic product modeling language. The product model descriptions are converted into formal descriptions with axioms so that reasoners can check the consistency of the formal descriptions and infer new knowledge based on the descriptions and their instances, i.e., information about physical products. In order to develop the converter and reasoners, the syntax and semantics of the product modeling language need to be defined. In this paper, the structure of the modeling framework and the abstract syntax and semantics of the product modeling language are proposed. A concrete syntax and editing interface for the product modeling language are under current development. Although needed to make the language comfortable for engineers not trained in ontology, they are out of scope for this paper.

The framework includes a generic product modeling language. The language enables product designers to define their product models from an engineering point of view while exploiting the benefits of ontology languages. The product modeling language consists of generic product domain concepts and relationships, such as 'artifact', 'behavior', and their relationships (explained later in the paper), which can guide product designers in building their product-specific information models, such as models of cars, airplanes, ships, etc. The language extends existing work on ontological product modeling languages [Bock 2009] to support product model

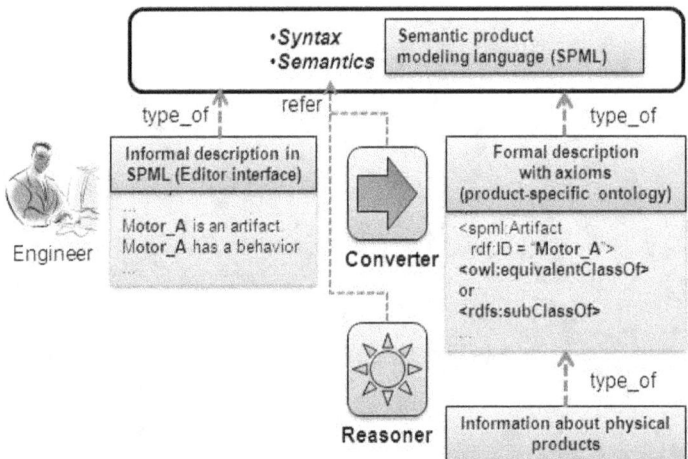

Figure 1. A high level view of the product modeling framework.

verification as in the Core Product Model 2 (CPM2), a product modeling language, which also contains generic product concepts and relationships [Fenves 2005].

The product modeling language is specialized from an ontology language, while product models are represented as instances of the language. Thereby, product designers can share and understand the semantics of the product information and design knowledge. In addition, the framework clarifies the different meanings of the product information modeling layers, so that: (1) the generic product model is used as the product modeling language; (2) product-specific design models can be represented in the product modeling language; and (3) information about physical products can be represented as instances of the product-specific models.

This paper is organized as follows. Section 2 reviews previous research on product information models and ontological multi-layered product modeling architectures. Section 3 presents an overview of the proposed multi-layered product modeling framework, including the generic product model. Section 4 addresses the concepts and relationships in the integrated generic product model, and their semantics. Section 5 describes the interaction mechanisms within the multi-layered product modeling framework. Section 6 illustrates the proposed model with an example case. Section 7 gives suggestions for future work and also contains the conclusions of this paper.

2. Previous Research

Product information models have evolved as new information modeling representations have emerged. Recently, product information models for product lifecycle management have adapted ontological representations to express the semantics of the information models. Researchers have also proposed multi-layered frameworks in order to manage relationships between the product information at different abstraction levels. These approaches to product information modeling are reviewed in this section.

2.1 Product information models

In the early 1990's, several product information models were developed using structured or object-oriented representations. Among these, the Standard for the Exchange of Product Model Data (STEP) is a comprehensive standard, covering a wide range of manufacturing product data, both generic (i.e., generic and integrated resources) and domain-specific (i.e., application protocols) [ISO 10303-1 1994]. STEP uses the EXPRESS language to represent information models [ISO 10303-11 2004]. CONGEN and SHARED are object-oriented information models intended to capture engineering knowledge from the most basic physical principles through domain-specific principles, including commonly used assemblies of physical systems [Gorti 1996], [Gorti 1998]. Other object-oriented product or process models have been developed by [Gu 1994], [Chen 1997], [Chep 1999], and others. The Unified Modeling Language (UML) [OMG 2001] has also been used to represent information models, as in the MOKA methodology for product design modeling and development of knowledge-based engineering applications [Stokes 2001].

2.2 Ontological representations

As information sharing for collaborative product development became important by the end of the 1990's, semantic description issues have become crucial. Therefore, ontological representations began to be introduced into product information modeling. Guarino et al. proposed fundamental theories related to product information in order to specify the semantics of concepts in STEP [Guarino 1997]. The Product Semantic Representation Language (PSRL) was developed for the exchange of product data semantics between different domains [Patil 2005]. PSRL adopted CPM as the product model and used the DAML+OIL ontology language

[Horrocks 2001] for representation. Lin et al. defined an ontology for managing customers' requirements, product specifications and relationships among them in first-order logic [Lin 1996]. Borst and Akkermans proposed an engineering ontology based on the PHYSYS ontology to specifically and clearly represent product knowledge [Borst 1997]. The PHYSYS ontology includes three conceptual viewpoints on physical systems: system layout, physical processes underlying behavior, and descriptive mathematical relationships [Borst 1997]. The ontology was represented in KIF (Knowledge Interchange Format) [Genesereth 1992]. Kitamura designed a functional concept ontology, which provides a vocabulary for functional representation [Kitamura 2002]. Kim et al. defined an ontology of assemblies for enhancing an assembly relationship model (ARM) [Kim 2006]. The assembly ontology represents engineering, spatial, assembly, and joining relationships and is implemented using both the web ontology language (OWL) [McGuinness 2004] and semantic web rule language (SWRL)[Horrocks 2004].

2.3   Multi-layered product modeling frameworks

Ontology representations, such as first-order logic [Brachman 2004b], description logic [Brachman 2004a], and OWL, have been widely used for representing formal descriptions of ontological components such as concepts and relationships. However, it is a heavy burden on a product designer to understand these formalisms and to be able to use them to represent product models. Therefore, specialized product modeling languages are necessary so that product designers can build and use their product models on top of generic product domain concepts that are independent of specific product domains. Collaborative design environments also need product-specific ontologies, namely, sets of concepts, relationships, and constraints related to a specific product domain such as 'car', 'axle', or 'bolt,' defined using a specialized product modeling language. The resulting product-specific ontologies have instances, which have measured values of the design parameters. Finally, collaborative product design environments need integrated semantics of both the generic product modeling language and the product-specific ontologies.

Since the early 2000's, interest in product modeling has turned to the support of Product Lifecycle Management (PLM). PLM deals with product information at many different levels of abstraction. Therefore, interest turned not only to sharing product information but also to considering different abstraction levels of information during a lifecycle of the product. PLM requires representation of data at multiple levels of abstraction in order to integrate systems across different lifecycle stages. This need gave rise to multi-layered approaches for integrated models of product lifecycle information [Srinivasan 2009]. Product ontology modeling research adopted multi-layer approaches to clarify semantics of product ontologies in different levels of abstraction.

Edmond *et al.* proposed algorithms for developing specific product ontologies in order to reuse product data in a product data management system for evaluating alternative design [Edmond 2007]. Lee et al. proposed a multi-layered ontology architecture for collaborative enterprises [Lee 2008], in which representation layers and domain modeling layers are separated, and adopted the model driven architecture (MDA) [OMG 2007] for the representation of layers. The modeling layers included: a domain independent layer; a domain dependent layer; and a domain specific layer. The domain modeling layers could be built using a top-level ontology such as the suggested upper merged ontology (SUMO) [Niles 2001]. Lee and Suh also proposed an ontology-based four-layered product knowledge framework to manage the integrity of the comprehensive product knowledge [Lee 2009]. Product ontologies were classified into four types: a product context model; a product specific model; a product planning model; and a product manufacturing model. The ISO-15926 standard for Life Cycle Data for Process Plants also had a multi-layered knowledge framework for plant process information and used the OWL-Full language to express the multi-layered plant ontologies [Leal 2005]. Yang et al. proposed a multi-layered ontology architecture for product configuration consisting of four layers: a representation layer; a meta-model layer; a model layer; and an instance layer [Yang 2008].

The previous studies reviewed here all did not provide a modeling language for engineers. Although they exploited ontological reasoning capability in their models, they did not explain how engineers can use the modeling language and exploit the reasoning capability.

2.4 Related NIST efforts

Significant work in product modeling languages has been developed by the Design Process Group at National Institute of Standards and Technology (NIST). In particular, CPM [Fenves 2002], CPM2 [Fenves 2005], Open Assembly Model (OAM) [Rachuri 2006], and ontological product modeling language (OPML) [Bock 2009], provide product information models with generic terms such as 'artifact', 'behavior,' and 'form'. CPM and OPML were developed to represent a generic product modeling language, while OAM is an information model specialized from CPM2 to express geometric constraints, kinematics, and tolerance in assemblies.

CPM2 was conceived as a representation for product development information and can form the basis of future systems that provide improved interoperability among software tools [Szykman 2001a]. CPM focused on an artifact representation that encompasses a range of engineering design concepts beyond the artifact's geometry, including function, form, behavior, and material, as well as physical and functional decompositions, mappings between function and form, and various kinds of relationships among these concepts. CPM2 defines generic product domain concepts and relationships, represented in the Unified Modeling Language (UML). CPM2 was not defined in a multi-layered product modeling framework. Although the CPM2 report suggests an intermediate model to express product-specific properties, CPM2 is limited in its ability of checking the consistency of the product-specific models according to the restrictions in CPM2.

OPML adapted and extended portions of CPM2 in a multi-layered modeling architecture generating product models represented as specializations of OWL. OPML adopts MDA in order to clarify the meanings of its multiple layers. MDA consists of four layers labeled M0, M1, M2, and M3. MDA uses instantiation relationships to express relationships between two adjacent layers. The M0 layer consists of individuals that can have no further instantiations. The M1 layer consists of models that classify individuals. The M2 layer consists of a modeling language, such as UML, and consists of shorthand expressions for the semantics of the model. The M3 layer comprises a meta-language, such as meta-object facility (MOF) [OMG 2003], for defining the modeling languages. OPML defines its product modeling language in M2, and the language is specialized from OWL. This enables the product modeling language to have the capabilities of ontology languages, such as taxonomies, which are available to engineers in their own terminology, rather than in those of ontology languages such as OWL. OPML supports modeling primitives for behavior, such as objects involved in behaviors, which CPM2 did not provide beyond artifact behaviors. In particular, OPML supports the concept of the Environment, the part of the universe that uses, interacts with, or is affected by the artifact being designed, but is beyond the designer's control. The current effort augments OPML with additional aspects of CPM2, in particular the verification of product behavior.

3. The multi-layered product information modeling framework

The proposed framework contains three layers for ontological product modeling, namely: the ontological product modeling language (M2), product-specific ontological models (M1), and physical item information (M0). Figure 2 shows the three layers and the relationships among them.[1]

---

[1] UML notations will be used as much as possible for figures in this paper.

The first layer (M2) is the modeling language. A semantics-based product modeling language (SPML) is proposed at this layer. As shown in Figure 2, the concepts and relationships in SPML are specialized from OWL classes, and the syntax and semantics of SPML inherit the syntax and semantics of OWL. The semantics of SPML need to be specified further because its classes and relationships require more specialized semantics for the domain of products. Since OWL can be a meta-modeling language to express semantics of SPML at M2, OWL is used to represent the axioms explicitly. For example, 'Artifact' and 'Designed Behavior' classes in SPML have different axioms. Although both classes are sub-classes of owl:Class[2], only the 'Artifact' class has an axiom that it must have at least one relationship with 'Designed Behavior.' Specifically, the semantics of 'Artifact' constrains an artifact to have at least one 'Designed Behavior.'

The second layer (M1) is for product-specific ontological models. A product-specific model at M1 holds representative information about a particular product. It consists of product-specific concepts and relationships such as artifacts, behaviors, forms, and structures of a specific product, including attributes and their (required or designed) values. The concepts and relationships are defined by product designers, as instances of SPML, so that they can be checked by a reasoner to determine their conformity to the axioms in SPML (this is shown in the figure as Conformance). For instance, if a 'Motor' concept is defined as an instance of the 'Artifact' class and it does not have a relationship with any designed-behavior, a reasoner can find inconsistencies by checking the above axiom of the 'Artifact' class. If the concepts and relationships at M1 do not create any inconsistency with SPML, they are valid, and their axioms can be added or inferred. Most axioms at M1 can be defined by domain experts, but some of the axioms can be inferred from axioms of the product modeling language at M2.

The bottom layer (M0) is for physical product information. The information at M0 represents information about physical products observed at a certain time or space, or simulations of these. The information can be different from the product designers' intent or expectation. Physical product information needs to be related to the original design models, which may include

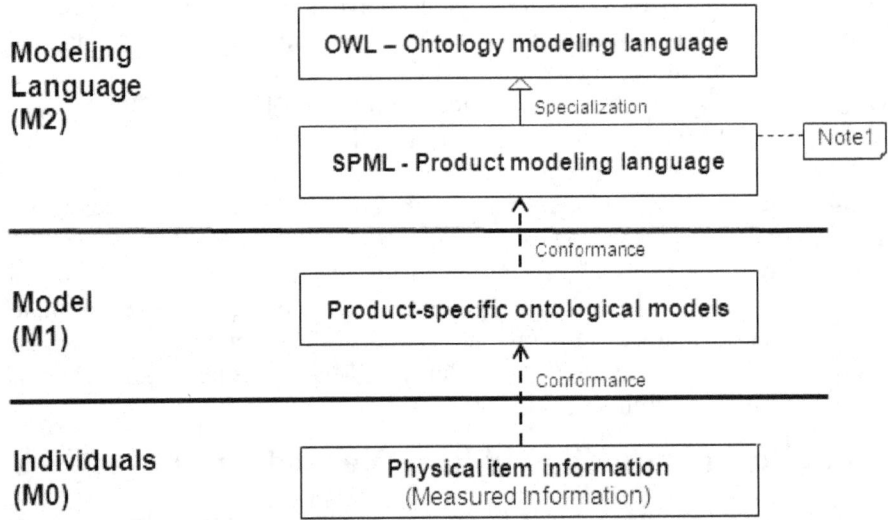

Note1: The SPML at M2 uses OWL as a meta-modeling language to express its axioms.

Figure 2. The multi-layered product information modeling framework.

---

[2] We use a prefix notation to represent a namespace of ontology, which the class belongs to. The 'owl', 'cpm2', 'opml', and 'spml' prefixes are used in this paper to represent namespaces of OWL, CPM2, OPML, and SPML ontology, respectively. In order to avoid naming conflicts, class names are expressed as '*prefix:local-class-name.*'

requirements as well as product designers' intent and plan. For example, a physical product in M0 needs to be related to the maintenance policy and geometry information described in the design model in M1.

The relationship between M0 and M1 is particularly important when the lifetime of the manufactured product is so long that information in the physical product may change several times, as in the case of ships, aircraft, and buildings. The conformance relationship in ontology modeling is better at expressing this relationship than the instantiation relationship in object-oriented modeling.

The conformance relationship is a relationship between an individual and a class in an ontological modeling perspective. Individuals can exist without their specific classes, so their attributes are not dependent on specific classes. A conformance relation can be established between an individual and a class by an inference engine if the information declared for the individual satisfies the definition of the class. There are other terms such as 'instance of' and 'type of' (used interchangeably in the literature). In this paper, these terms are distinguished with the term 'conforms to' to specifically mean that the instances are checked logically with reasoners to be consistent with the class's definitions. For example, an individual can be defined by engineers as an instance of a class but it may or may not be conformed to the class.

A physical product at M0 can conform to several product models at M1 such as a requirement model, a conceptual design model, an engineering model, etc. Since a physical product has detailed information, it can have more attributes than one of its product models at M1. Definitions at the M1 layer can be used to infer the conformance relationships between the M1 and M0 layers. A detailed description of the interaction between the M1 and M0 layers will be given in Section 5.

4. The Product Modeling Language: SPML

This section describes the classes and relations of the product modeling language at the M2 layer, in short, the SPML classes. Section 4.1 describes how SPML is specialized from OWL. Section 4.2 specifies the SPML classes, their definitions, and their constraints.

4.1 SPML and OWL

SPML uses OWL for its base language, while OWL is based on Resource Description Framework (RDF) [Beckett 2004] and RDF Schema [Brickley 2004], in short, RDF(S). Therefore, SPML classes are specialized from primitives in OWL, many of which are adopted or specialized from RDF(S) primitives. SPML inherits OWL semantics through the specialization relationship. In addition, SPML classes have axioms to specify their meanings explicitly. The axioms are also described in OWL, so that they can provide OWL syntax describing specific SPML product models at M1.

OWL provides three increasingly expressive sub-languages: OWL-Lite, OWL-DL, and OWL-Full. SPML is defined by specializing OWL, which technically requires OWL-Full. Even so, description logic reasoners can operate on models defined in SPML because SPML does not modify OWL semantics or require expressivity beyond OWL-DL.

Figure 3 shows the relationships between the SPML classes and the OWL primitives. The 'spml:Class' is the top class in SPML, and it is a sub-class of 'owl:Class.' Sub-classes of the 'spml:Class' will be defined in the following sub-section.

4.2 SPML classes

For the remainder of this sub-section, the "Arial" bold font is used to avoid repeating usage of the 'spml:' prefix. For example, **Class** means spml:Class.

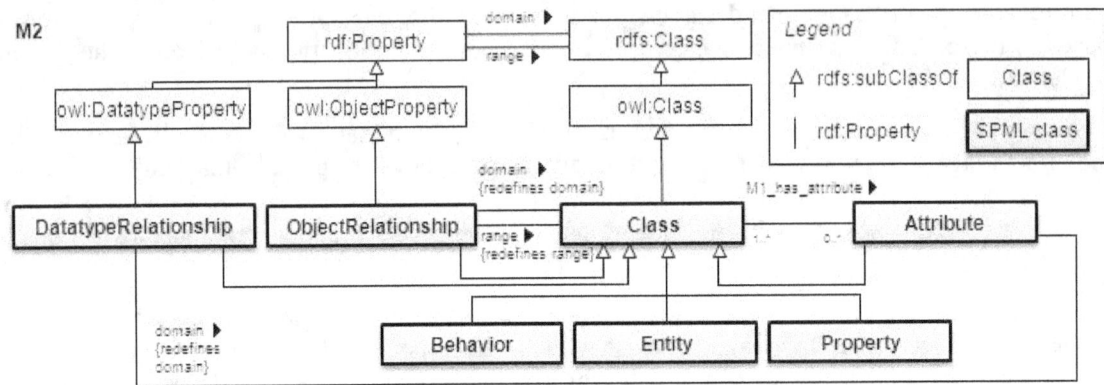

Figure 3. Relationships between OWL and SPML classes.

4.2.1 Attribute and DatatypeRelationship classes

Attribute is a class that describes other classes with literal values. For example, the attributes 'water-flow speed' and 'color' describe a 'water-bottle' product model with their literal values such as '50 cc/sec' and 'blue', respectively. **DatatypeRelationship** is a sub-class of owl:DatatypeProperty. It has sub-classes such as **has_value**, **has_datatype**, and **has_unit**. The domain of **DatatypeRelationship** is **Attribute**. The range of **DatatypeRelationship** is either literal values or a class restricting literal values. The literal values can be either text strings or individuals in other imported ontologies. If a literal value is an individual of an imported ontology, it must have a namespace. For example, if 'blue' is an individual in an imported 'http://ontology/standard_color' ontology, the value of the 'color' attribute can be expressed as 'http://ontology/standard_color#blue'. If there is a short-hand prefix for the namespace such as 'clr', the color can be expressed like 'clr:blue.' The data restriction class can express data restrictions such as 'integer value between 1 and 10', or 'literal value among green, yellow, and red.' In OWL 2.0, DatatypeRestriction class and DataOneOf class are defined to specify those data restrictions. SPML in this paper expresses data restrictions informally using literal values, but formal expressions for data restrictions will be incorporated to SPML after OWL 2.0 becomes a recommended standard.

Attribute and **DatatypeRelationship** cannot have attributes, but SPML classes other than **Attribute** and **DatatypeRelationship** can have as many attributes as needed in order to describe themselves. This restriction is defined as a domain restriction of the **has_attribute** relationship though it is not depicted in Figure 3. The domain restriction is defined as a union of SPML classes except **Attribute** and **DatatypeRelationship**. An attribute cannot exist without a class owning it, so every attribute has at least one relationship with a class. Sometimes, an attribute can be shared by many classes. For example, a 'color' attribute can be shared by a product and its components in order to keep the consistency of color.

Figure 4 shows how to use **Attribute** and **DatatypeRelationship** in the proposed multi-layered framework. In terms of product modeling, concepts of M1 can be classified into two classes; 1) an attribute class assigning values, and 2) a class which can have an attribute class. Thus, two classes are pre-defined at M1, namely, 'M1_Class' and 'M1_Attribute', which are instances of **Class** and **Attribute**, respectively. Every class at M1 layer is a sub-class of either **M1_Class** or **M1_Attribute**.

Relationships between classes at M1 are already defined in SPML. For instance, the **has_attribute** is defined as a relationship between **Class** and **Attribute** in SPML. The relationships between **Attribute** and rdfs:Literal are also defined in SPML as

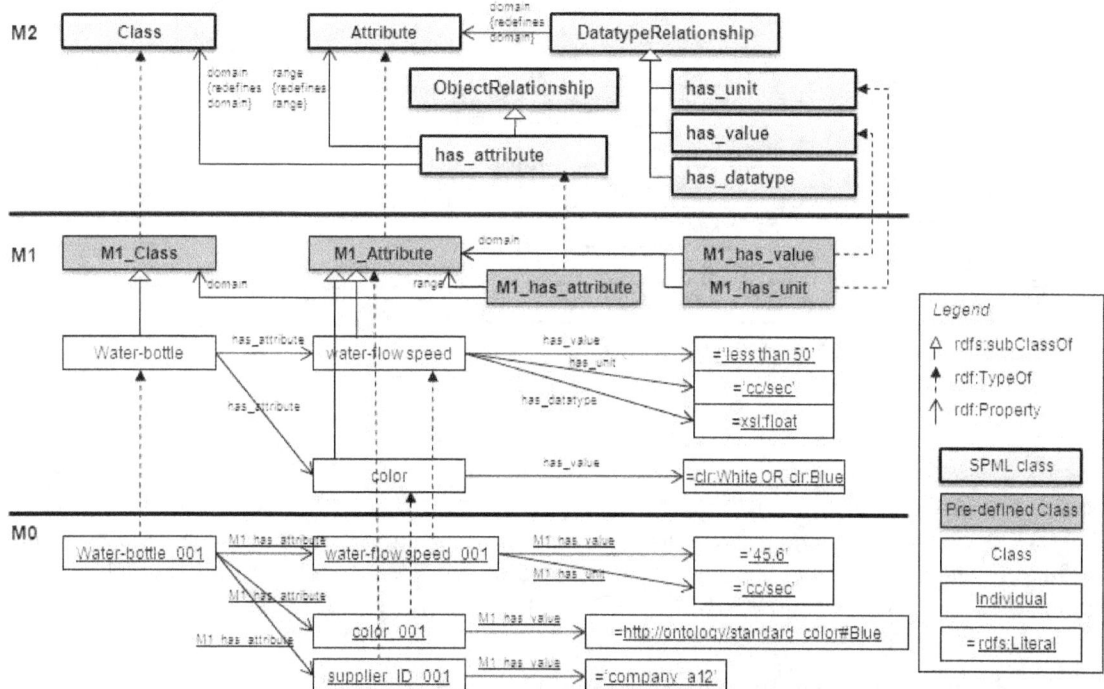

Figure 4. Example of **Attribute** and **DatatypeRelationship** in multi-layers.

DatatypeRelationship. Every **M1_Attribute** class can have literal values through the sub-relationships of **DatatypeRelationship** such as **has_value**, **has_datatype**, and **has_unit**.

Meanwhile, every individual at M0 is an instance of either 'M1_Class' or 'M1_Attribute.' Some individuals at M0 can be instances of other classes at M1 if the 'rdf:Type' relationship between the individual and the class is either defined by users or inferred by a reasoning engine. The relationships between individuals at M0 should be defined at M1. Since the relationship between an individual and its attribute does not change according to a specific product model at M1, 'M1_has_attribute' relationship is pre-defined at M1. 'M1_has_value' and 'M1_has_unit' relationships are also pre-defined at M1 to represent the relationship between an attribute and its literal values at M0.

Attribute values at M1 can describe product models at M1, so that they can have a range or enumeration constraint to restrict attribute values at M0. For instance, 'Water-bottle' class in Figure 4 has two attributes which have range and enumeration constraints. The 'Water-bottle' class, then, can be defined as a class which has two attributes, 'water-flow speed' and 'color,' which have a value range and enumeration constraint, respectively. The definition of the 'Water-bottle' can be used as a membership rule to check its conformance of individuals at M0. Attribute values at M0 have specific values, but they cannot have a range and enumeration constraint because their values belong to physical items at M0.

Since SPML is a generic product modeling language at M2, it does not contain predefined attributes that might be relevant only in specific domains (e.g., attributes of mechanical or electronic devices) or in specific objects (e.g., attributes specific to form or behavior).

4.2.2   ObjectRelationship classes

ObjectRelationship represents relationships between two classes. It is derived from the 'owl:ObjectProperty', and its domain and range is limited to **Class**. Only **DatatypeRelationship** is excluded from the domain and range class because **ObjectRelationship** defines relationships

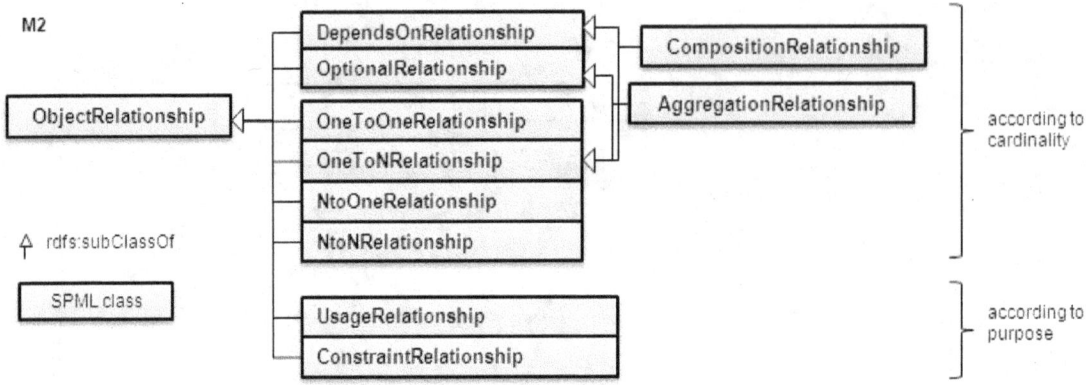

Figure 5. ObjectRelationship class hierarchy.

only between the five classes **Behavior**, **Entity**, **Property**, **ObjectRelationship**, and **Attribute**. **ObjectRelationship** is further specialized into sub-relationships according to the relationship's cardinality and specific purpose. The sub-relationships provide pre-defined terms which can help engineers to define semantics of their own relationships. Figure 5 shows the relationship hierarchy graphically.

1) ObjectRelationship classification according to cardinality.

Cardinality means a measure of the possible number of instances of a concept for a relationship. It can be represented with minimum and maximum number, i.e. (*min*, *max*), *min* $\in \{0, 1\}$, *max* $\in \{1, N\}$. For example, if the geometry class has a relationship 'is_geometry_of' to the artifact class, the cardinality of the geometry class for the relationship should be (1,N) because every geometry must describe at least one artifact, and can be the geometry of many artifacts in the product modeling context. The inverse of the relationship is 'has_geometry'; its cardinality for the artifact class should be (0,N) because some artifacts might not have a geometry but can also have many geometries.

Cardinality of a concept is a crucial axiom for maintaining the consistency of a product model. However, it may be difficult for engineers to understand the meaning of cardinality. For the above example, it might be better understandable for engineers that a geometry cannot exist without an artifact, but that an artifact has an optional geometry, and some of geometries and artifacts can have the relationship multiple times. These axioms can be formally defined for the relationships using the proposed sub-relationships of **ObjectRelationship**.

DependsOnRelationship expresses a relationship between two classes in which one class cannot exist without the other class. **OptionalRelationship** expresses a relationship between two classes in which one class can exist without another class. **OneToOneRelationship**, **OneToNRelationship**, **NtoOneRelationship**, and **NtoNRelationship** are defined according to the maximum cardinalities of the relationships and their inverses.

For formal definitions of the sub-relationships, the following functions are defined. If a relationship, R, is a relationship from a domain class, C, to a range class, D, the minimum and maximum cardinality of R for the class C is expressed as $MinCard(R) = x$, $MaxCard(R) = y$, $Card(R) = (x, y)$, for $x \in \{0, 1\}$, $y \in \{1, N\}$. If there is an inverse relationship 'R-' of the relationship R, its cardinality is expressed as $MinCard(R\text{-}) = j$, $MaxCard(R\text{-}) = k$, $Card(R\text{-}) = (j,k)$, for $j \in \{0, 1\}$, $k \in \{1, N\}$. For example, if an **ObjectRelationship** R is an **NtoNRelationship**, it means that there is an inverse relationship 'R-', $MaxCard(R) = N$, and $MaxCard(R\text{-}) = N$. A **DependsOnRelationship**, R, means $MinCard(R) = 1$. An **OptionalRelationship**, R, means

MinCard(R) = 0.

The 'is_geometry_of' relationship can now be defined as a sub-relationship of **DependsOnRelationship** and **NtoNRelationship**, and the 'has_geometry' relationship can be defined as a sub-relationship of **OptionalRelationship** and **NtoNRelationship**.

A structure relationship is frequently used in product modeling. It represents a relationship between two classes in which one class contains another class. It is a sub-relationship of **OneToNRelationship**, but its minimum cardinality can be either 0 or 1 depending on its applications. Two relationships, **AggregationRelationship** and **CompositionRelationship**, are defined to provide pre-defined terms for structure relationships. **AggregationRelationship** means *Card*(R) = (0,1) and *Card*(R-) = (0,N), so that it is a sub-relationship of **OneToNRelationship** and **OptionalRelationship**. **CompositionRelationship** means *Card*(R) = (1,1) and *Card*(R-) = (0,N), so that it is a sub-relationship of **OneToNRelationship** and **DependsOnRelationship**.

2) ObjectRelationship classification according to its specific purpose.

There are two sub-relationships of **ObjectRelationship**, namely, **UsageRelationship** and **ConstraintRelationship**. They are special relationships which require additional functions to achieve their purpose. **UsageRelationship** is a relationship to express usage of a specific class when that class is used in different ways. For example, in a car, an axle can be used in two different ways: front-axle and rear-axle. If a designer wants to define the two different usages of an axle, the **UsageRelationship** is used between the "source" axle class and the two "target" axle classes. **UsageRelationship** should provide a function which makes the two "target" axle classes inherit the relationships and attributes of the "source" axle class. A designer can define additional attributes for the front-axle class because the front-axle needs to be connected to an engine. So, **UsageRelationship** is a specialization relationship among instances of **Behavior**, **Entity**, and **Property**, but its domain and range must be instances of the same SPML class.

ConstraintRelationship is a relationship describing restrictions such as expert's rules or mathematical functions that must hold in all cases. For example, a cylinder and a hole have the constraint relationship that the diameter of the cylinder must be less than the diameter of the hole, so that the cylinder can be inserted into the hole. The relationship can be represented either between the cylinder and the hole or between the diameter of the cylinder and the diameter of the hole. Thus, **ConstraintRelationship** is a relationship either among instances of **Behavior**, **Entity**, and **Property**, or among instances of **Attribute**. In addition, it requires additional modules to execute rules or functions expressed with a constraint.

Each sub-relationship has further sub-relationships, which are defined in the SPML relationships. For example, since an 'is_involved_in' relationship between **Entity** and **Behavior** includes the meaning that **Behavior** cannot exist without a related **Entity** in the context of product-modeling, it is a sub-relationship of the **DependsOnRelationship**.

4.2.3 Entity, Behavior, and Property classes

Entity, **Behavior**, and **Property** are crucial concepts for building product-specific models. They have relationships among themselves, and have further sub-classes which inherit the relationships. Figure 6 shows the classes and relationships graphically. Their sub-classes will be described in the following sub-sections.

Entity represents things that can be described with **Behavior** and **Property**. **Entity** can be involved in some **Behavior**. **Behavior** is a dynamic aspect of one or more **Entities**. A dynamic aspect involves the notion of time in its description. For example, 'sitting on a chair,' and 'maintaining color' are behaviors because they occur in a time interval.

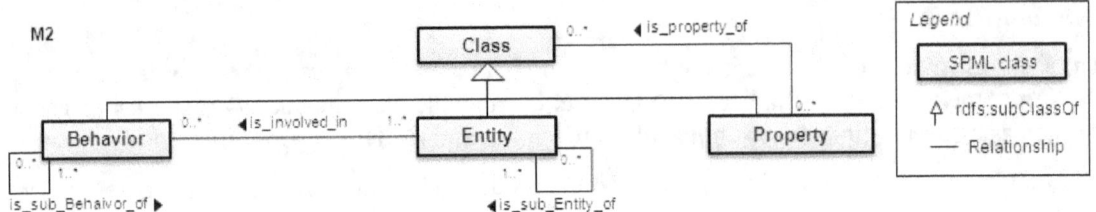

Figure 6. Entity, Behavior, and Property classes.

Property represents things that describe **Class**, excluding the dynamics of the **Class** represented by **Behavior**. **Property** must describe either **Entity** or **Behavior** so instances of it cannot exist without at least one 'is_property_of' relationship to an instance of either **Entity** or **Behavior**. **Property** is different from **Attribute** because properties can be further described by attributes while **Attribute** cannot have attributes. For example, 'motor cylinder' property (geometry) of an 'electronic motor' can describe with its attributes such as 'diameter' and 'length.' However, attributes such as 'diameter' and 'length' cannot be further described by other attributes in SPML.

Behavior and **Entity** have reflexive structure relationship for their containment hierarchy. Their sub-classes inherit the relationship, but there are two rules for inheritance. The first rule is that the inherited structure relationships have their own names. For example, the inherited structure relationship of **Artifact** is defined as the 'is_sub_Artifact_of' relationship while the name of the structure relationship of **Entity** is 'is_sub_Entity_of'. The second rule is that the range of the structure relationship of a sub-class is limited to the sub-class itself. For example, the 'is_sub_Artifact_of' relationship is not a relationship between **Artifact** and **Entity**, but a relationship between two **Artifact**s.

4.2.3.1 Entity classes

Figure 7 shows the class hierarchy of **Entity**. **Entity** is divided into **ExternalEntity** and **SpecifiedEntity**, and **SpecifiedEntity** is divided further into **Artifact** and **Feature**. Some sub-

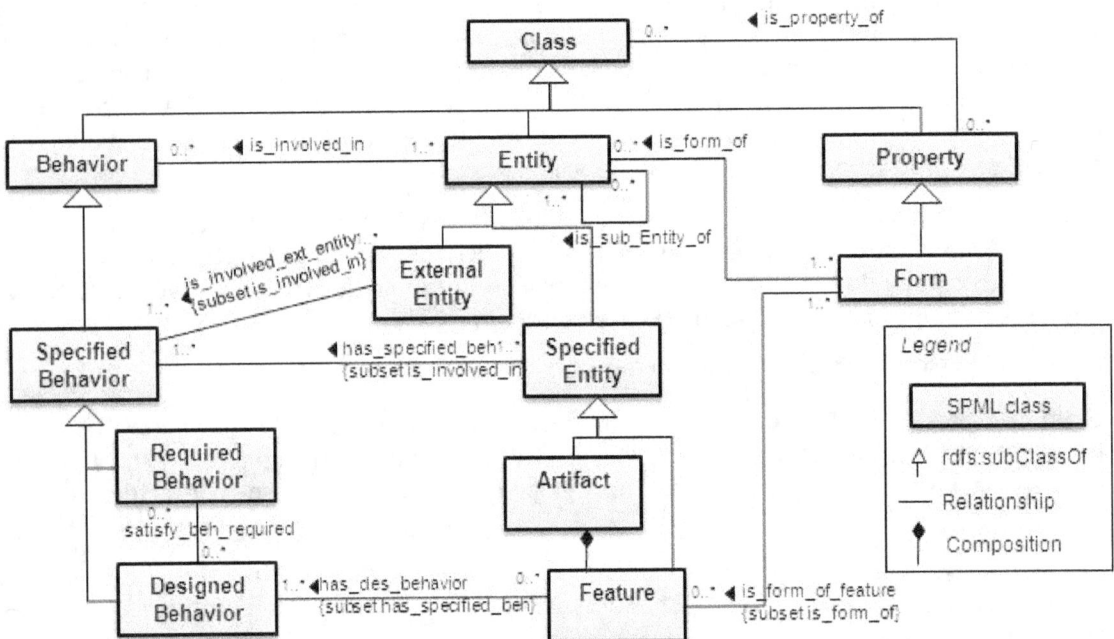

Figure 7. Entity hierarchy.

classes of **Behavior** and **Property** are shown together to explain sub-classes of **Entity**.

ExternalEntity is a kind of **Entity** that interacts with **Artifact** in a context of use, which is a required behavior. The required behavior identifies some entities participating in it as the external entities. The external entities interact with the entity being specified (the artifact), which is also involved in the required behavior. For example, person's hand and mouth, and water can be external entities for designing a water-bottle because they give required behaviors to the water-bottle design.

SpecifiedEntity is a kind of **Entity** that is specified with **SpecifiedBehavior** and **Form**. **Artifact** and **Feature** are sub-classes of **SpecifiedEntity**. A designed entity must be involved in at least one specified behavior (either required behavior or designed behavior) and have at least one form. For example, a water-bottle can be a designed entity that has a specified behavior 'containing water' and a material (a subclass of form) 'plastic.'

Artifact is a kind of **SpecifiedEntity** which is designed, as opposed to entities that are naturally occurring. Artifacts must be involved in at least one specified behavior. A required behavior for an artifact comes from external entities that are part of the universe of discourse that uses or interacts with the artifact. **Artifact** and **ExternalEntity** are not disjoint because an artifact can be an external entity for another artifact. For instance, a 'desk' can be an external entity for a 'chair' design, while a 'chair' can be an external entity for a 'desk.'

Feature is a kind of **SpecifiedEntity** which is a portion of an artifact. A feature has relationships with specific forms and behaviors of its artifact to specify relationships between the specific forms and behaviors. For example, the 'bottle-neck' of a 'water-bottle' can be a feature the form of which is a 'through-hole,' and the designed behavior of which is 'guiding water-flow.' The relationship between **Artifact** and **Feature** is defined as a composite relationship because they have a structural relationship and a feature cannot exist without an artifact.

4.2.3.2 Behavior classes

Figure 8 shows the class hierarchy of the **Behavior** class. Some sub-classes of **Entity** and **Property** are included in the figure to explain **Behavior** sub-classes. Behaviors are classified into two direct sub-classes: **SpecifiedBehavior** and **TestBehavior**.

SpecifiedBehavior is a kind of **Behavior** specifying dynamic aspects of entities, which are invariant. It is further specialized into **RequiredBehavior** and **DesignedBehavior**.

RequiredBehavior describes external entities' dynamics, which affect artifact design. Required behaviors are classified into two classes.

- **InformalRequiredBehavior** is a behavioral description of the dynamics of the external entities surrounding artifacts. The description explains behaviors of the external entities informally, and provides initial data for the analysis of interactions between external entities and artifacts. For example, 'Person is drinking water' is an example of informal required behavior. A designer can start to think about an artifact like 'water-bottle' and its interactions with external entities, such as 'person' and 'water', based on the description. A required behavior can have sub-behaviors. Sub-behaviors are described with more specific entities or verbs. For example, the above example can have sub-behaviors: 'Hand tilts a water-bottle' and 'Mouth contacts a water-bottle.'

- **FormalRequiredBehavior** explicitly specifies external entities, artifacts, and their interactions. A formal required behavior can be derived from an informal required behavior. While an informal required behavior is expressed with a sentence, a formal required behavior is expressed with a structured sentence and attributes. A structured sentence consists of a subject, verb, and object [Weissman 2009]. Entities can be used as a subject or object. From the previous example, 'person,' 'hand,' 'mouth,' and 'water' are defined as external entities, and a 'water-bottle' is defined as an artifact. Verb taxonomy is required to specify verbs. For instance, [Hirtz 2002] and [Kitamura 2002] defined verb taxonomies to describe engineering behaviors and functions, respectively. From the previous example, 'drink,' 'tilt,' and 'contact' are verbs to describe the required behaviors, and a formal required behavior 'FB01' can be expressed with a subject 'person', a verb 'drink', and an object 'water.' Attributes also needed to specify a formal required behavior. For instance, the 'FB01' formal required behavior has an attribute 'water flow-rate' whose value is 'more than 50 cc/sec.'

DesignedBehavior specifies behaviors of an artifact or feature, determined by product designers in response to formal required behaviors. It identifies some entities participating in it as specified entities (artifact and feature). The subject of its description should be an artifact or feature, while the subject of required behavior's description is an external entity. For example, 'Water-bottle provides water to mouth' is a designed behavior for the above required behavior example. A designed behavior can have specific attributes and their values that satisfy the attributes and values defined at corresponding required behaviors. For example, the 'water flow-rate' of the above designed behavior can have a value 'more than 60 cc/sec.'

Designed behaviors are defined to satisfy required behaviors. The relationship between **RequiredBehavior** and **DesignedBehavior**, 'satisfy_beh_required' relationship in Figure 8, means a specialization relationship. So, a designed behavior in the M1 layer can be described as a sub-class of required behaviors. In addition, artifacts involved in a designed behavior in the M1 layer should be a sub-class of another artifact that is involved in the required behaviors, or they can be a same class.

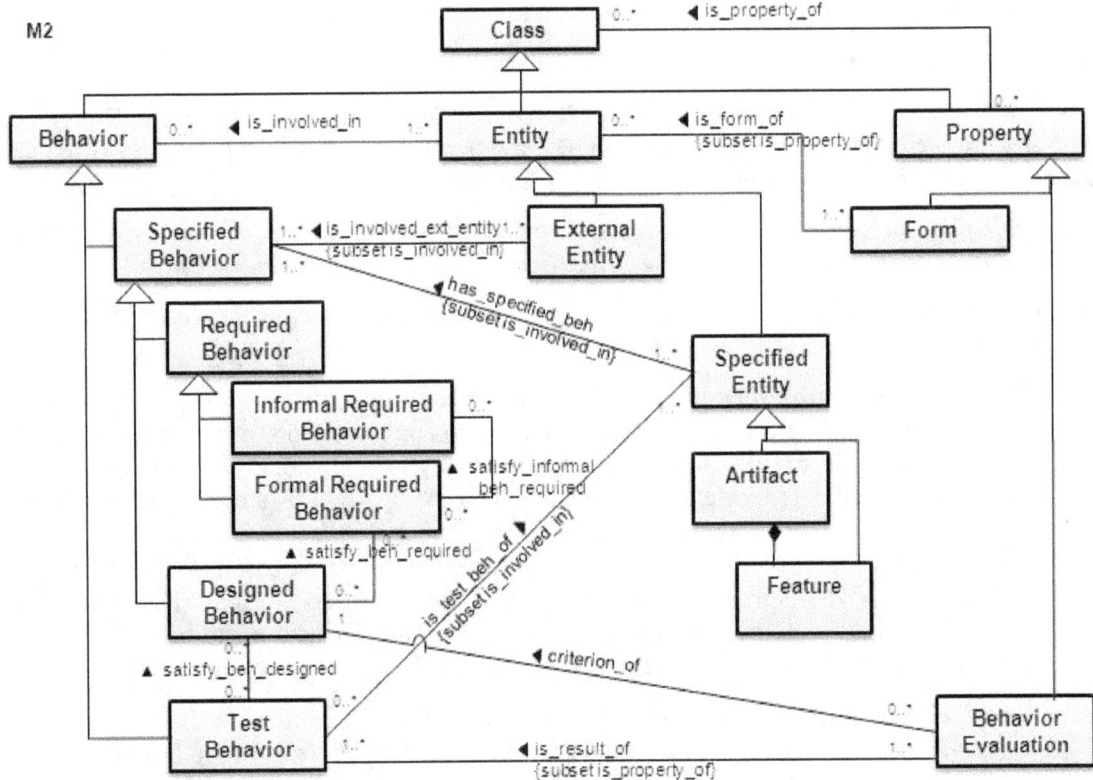

Figure 8. **Behavior** hierarchy.

TestBehavior is a behavior of an artifact or feature that can be observed after testing with a test method. External entities and designed entities can be involved in describing a test behavior, but a test behavior cannot exist without a related designed entity. **TestBehavior** is the observed behavior of the artifact or feature. It can be observed through test methods such as running mathematical models or simulation models, or testing physical prototypes or manufactured items. The test methods should be defined as an attribute of test behaviors at the M1 layer.

A test behavior of an artifact or feature should be compared to a designed behavior. It can satisfy the designed behavior if its observed behaviors are qualified for the designed behavior. Otherwise, it cannot satisfy the designed behavior. The evaluation results are recorded with **BehaviorEvaluation** class, which is a sub-class of **Property**. Conformance relationship between the M1 and M0 layer is used to evaluate test behaviors, which will be explained in Section 5.

4.2.3.3 Property classes

Figure 9 shows the class hierarchy of **Property**. The hierarchies of **Behavior** and **Entity** are also included to explain relationships with them.

Property has two sub-classes; **Form** and **BehaviorEvaluation**. Forms are properties of **Entity**, and behavior evaluations are properties of **TestBehavior**. Only those two sub-classes are defined in this paper, but the class hierarchy of **Property** can be expanded with more sub-classes in future works if product development domain requires more properties.

Form specifies properties of entities that explain geometry and material aspects of the entities. It has two sub-classes: **Geometry** and **Material**. **Geometry** is defined to describe the measurements of lines, angles, surfaces, solids, and relationships among them. **Material** describes the substances that entities can be made from.

The relationship between **Form** and **Entity**, 'is_form_of' relationship, is used to specify forms of entities at the M1 layer. The relationship means a specialization relationship at the M1 layer. For example, a 'Cylinder' geometry at M1 can be used to describe many artifact designs such as a cup,

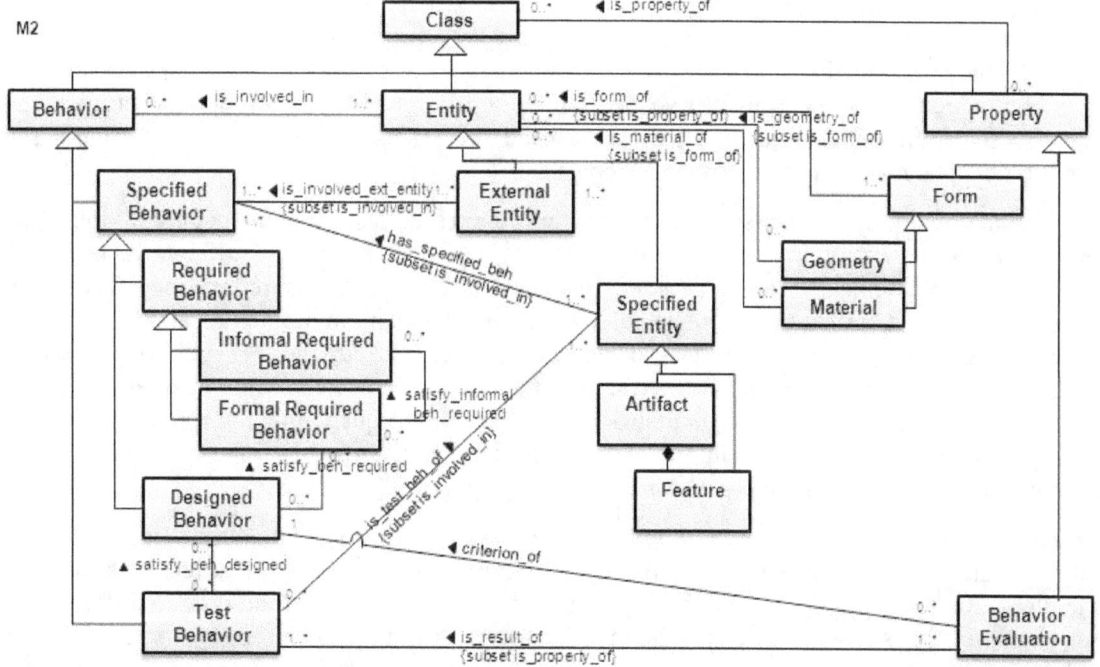

Figure 9.   Property hierarchy.

pipe, or drum artifact at M1. All instances of those artifacts at M0 are members of the 'Cylinder' geometry. So, the cup, pipe, and drum artifacts at M1 are sub-classes of the 'Cylinder' geometry. The specialization relationship is derived from the 'is_form_of' relationships between the artifacts and geometry classes at M1. If an engineer defines that 'Cylinder' geometry at M1 has the 'is_form_of' relationship with a 'Cup' artifact at M1, the semantic of the relationship should be defined as a specialization relationship [Bock 2009].

BehaviorEvaluation is a sub-class of **Property** and is used to record results of behavior tests. It has an attribute 'result' at the M1 layer to specify the test results such as 'satisfactory' or 'failure.'

5. Developing Product Models and Instances using SPML

SPML is an extension of OWL, which provides mechanisms for engineers to specify their models in this language. Using SPML at the layer M2 will allow engineers to write their product models at the M1 layer in this language (i.e., interaction between M2 and M1), which provides product-specific semantics developed in SPML (i.e., adding semantics to the product models). Once engineers defined product models using SPML, they can instantiate their product models and check conformance of the real world instances to the product models (i.e., interaction between M1 and M0).

5.1 Three layers

The three layers of the proposed framework are the product modeling language layer (M2), the layer of product-specific ontological models (M1), and the physical objects layer (M0).

First, the product modeling language layer (M2) includes classes and relationships to represent product-specific ontological models. It also includes axioms of the classes and relationships. The axioms specify meanings of the classes and relationships, and can be used to check syntactic consistency of the product specific model descriptions at M1.

Second, the product-specific ontological models (M1) are described in the product modeling language. A product-specific model includes product-specific classes and relationships. It represents information about behaviors, entities, and their properties, and structures of specific products, including attributes and values. The attribute values at M1 can be a range of values or enumeration constraint to express the values required or designed for an artifact or feature at M1. A product-specific ontological model at M1 can be specialized into sub-ontological models in order to describe further detailed product models.

The semantics of a product-specific model are expressed as product-specific axioms and definitions. The name of a class alone cannot capture the semantics sufficiently to enable engineers to communicate with each other. Axioms are required to ensure that the class's name corresponds with its semantics. For example, a 'motor' class can be defined as an artifact which has coils and magnets that convert electric energy into mechanical energy. A specialized motor for a specific company may have more specific definitions such as a motor which diameter is 50 ± 5 mm, and it requires 12 V electricity and produces 50 ± 5 Nm torque with 6000 rpm rotation speed. Most product-specific axioms should be defined by domain experts, but some of the axioms can be inferred from axioms of the product modeling language (M2).

Product-specific models often need to be integrated because the models represent only parts of an entire product. Integration is different from just putting information about different products in one place. Rather, it needs to be performed considering the semantics of the product information. For example, let us assume that the designed behavior of an impeller product is to make wind, and its definition is a combination of 'generate rotation energy' and 'transform rotation-energy to wind-energy'. If a motor and a fan model were combined into an impeller product model to achieve the designed behavior of an impeller, the designed behavior of a motor, fan, and impeller should be evaluated. The evaluation requires the semantics of each designed behavior. Another example is an integration of two product models using a specialization relationship. A 'motor_A' concept in conceptual design and a 'motor_B' concept in detail design can be integrated using a specialization relationship if 'motor_B' has all the information that 'motor_A' has in addition to information about its design.

Last, the physical information layer (M0) includes individuals and their relationships. Individuals have attributes and values so that they can represent information of physical products such as realized design prototypes, manufactured products, or products in use. They do not have axioms. An individual can conform to classes in product-specific ontological models (M1) if its information satisfies definitions of the classes. Definitions are axioms of the classes in product-specific ontological models (M1).

5.2   Developing product models (M2 -M1 interactions)

Engineers and inference systems perform the interaction between the M2 and M1 layers. Engineers use SPML (M2) to describe their product-specific ontological models (M1). Axioms of SPML provide OWL syntax for SPML, and inference systems can assist engineers by telling what classes and relationships are needed to be defined. Inference systems can also check syntactic consistency of engineers' descriptions at M1 based on the SPML syntax. For example, let us assume that there are SPML axioms like Figure 10-(a). The axioms are represented in the Manchester OWL syntax [Horridge 2006]. They specify every artifact at M1 must have at least one relationship 'has_form' with Form class. If an engineer defines a 'Motor' artifact class like Figure 10-(b), inference systems can check syntactic consistency of the description and tell what information is missing. Then, systems can provide templates for engineers to describe the missing information. The place underlined in Figure 10-(c) is where engineers need to fill the missing information.

5.3   Adding semantics in the product models

If a product model description at M1 satisfies the axioms of SPML, axioms for the product model description at M1 can be added. Axioms at the M1 layer are defined for each behavior, form, and entity.

A behavior can be described with its attributes and sub-behaviors. For example, let us assume that a designed behavior 'Rotating a fan' of a motor is described like Figure 11. A behavior can be

Index	SPML - OWL expressions

(a)
SPML axioms example
	Class: Artifact
	   SubClassOf: SpecifiedEntity
	
	Class: SpecifiedEntity
	   SubClassOf: Entity **and**
	   SubClassOf: (has_form **only** Form) **and**
	   SubClassOf: (has_form **some** Form)

(b) Engineer's initial description example	**<spml:Artifact** rdf:ID= "Motor">

(c)
Template example provided by inference systems
	<spml:Artifact rdf:ID= "Motor">
	   <spml:has_form rdf:ID= " ___ ">
	     <spml:Geometry rdf:ID= " ___ "/>
	     <spml:Material rdf:ID= " ___ "/>
	   </spml:has_form>
	</spml:Artifact>

Figure 10.   An example of interactions between the M2 and M1 layers.

```
<spml:DesignedBehavior rdf:ID= "Rotating_a_fan">
 <spml:specifies>
   <spml:Artifact rdf:ID= "Motor"/>
   <spml:ExternalEntity rdf:ID= "Fan" />
 </spml:specifies>
 <spml:M1_has_attribute>
     <spml:Attribute rdf:ID= "torque">
       <spml:M1_has_value>  [>50, <100]   </spml:M1_has_value>
       <spml:M1_has_datatype rdf:Resource= "xsd:integer"/>
       <spml:M1_has_unit rdf:Resource = "ut:Nm" />
     </spml:Attribute>
     <spml:Attribute rdf:ID= "rpm">
       <spml:M1_has_value>  [>3000, <5000]   </spml:M1_has_value>
       <spml:M1_has_datatype rdf:Resource= "xsd:integer"/>
       <spml:M1_has_unit rdf:Resource = "ut:rpm" />
     </spml:Attribute>
 </spml:M1_has_attribute>
 <spml:has_sub_behavior>
     <spml:DesignedBehavior rdf:ID= "Receive_electricity"/>
     <spml:DesignedBehavior rdf:ID= "Spin_axis"/>
 </spml:has_sub_behavior>
</spml:DesignedBehavior>
```

Figure 11.   A behavior description example at the M1 layer.

differentiated from other behaviors based on its attributes and sub-behaviors. So, the definition of the behavior can be generated from the attributes and sub-behaviors like Figure 12. The description in Figure 11 and axioms Figure 12 are now hard coded to show how SPML can be used by engineers and how semantics can be added into product models, but ideally would be generated automatically using an SPML editor user interface.

Inference systems require axiom generation rules in order to add axioms to the behavior descriptions. Axiom generation rules can be expressed or implemented in various ways. [Lee 2007] and [Liang 2008] showed implementation of rules using eXtensible Stylesheet Language Transformations (XSLT) [Clark 1999] and Java [Gosling 2005], respectively. They find patterns in a product description and generate axioms or definitions for the description.

The rules should be designed considering the axioms of SPML at the M2 layer. Then, axioms at the M1 layer can be generated automatically from the sentences defined by engineers. However, axioms generated by rules may not be sufficient to fully specify all the semantics of product models in M1. Especially, when the semantics concern engineering knowledge that is product

```
spml:DesignedBehavior: Rotating_a_fan
  EquivalentTo:
     (spml:M0_has_attribute only (torque or rpm))  and
     (spml:M0_has_attribute exactly 2)  and
     (spml:M0_has_attribute some ( torque and
                  (spml:M0_has_value some int[>50, <100])))  and        Axioms for an
     (spml:M0_has_attribute some ( rpm and                               attribute 'torque'
                  (spml:M0_has_value some int[>3000, <5000])))
     and
     (spml:has_sub_behavior only (Receive_electricity or Spin_axis)) and    Axioms for
     (spml:has_sub_behavior some Receive_electricity)  and                  sub-behaviors
     (spml:has_sub_behavior some Spin_axis)
```

Figure 12.   Axioms example for an attribute and sub-behaviors at the M1 layer.

specific, some axioms have to be generated manually by engineers in order to express the exact meanings of concepts. For example, if engineers know what attributes and sub-behaviors can discriminate the 'Rotating_a_fan' behavior from other behaviors, they can select attributes and sub-behaviors for the definition.

Axioms for form and entity descriptions in M1 can also be generated like behavior axioms. Since entities are described with their behaviors, axioms of entities can be also described using the axioms of the behaviors. For example, a 'Motor_A' artifact class can be defined as an artifact that must have a designed behavior 'Rotating_a_fan.' Then, the definition of the motor will refer the behavior, and the definition of the behaviors will be included in the definition of the motor.

Axioms for SPML relationships also need to be generated and added to the product model descriptions. Some SPML relationships are interpreted as specialization relationships such as 'satisfy' relationships among behaviors and 'is_form_of' relationships between entity and form.

If a designed behavior satisfies a required behavior, the attributes and sub-behaviors of the designed behavior should be more specific than those of the required behavior. A specialization relationship between two classes enables inference systems to verify the 'satisfy' relationship between behaviors.

An 'is_form_of' relationship between an entity and form class is also interpreted as a specialization relationship, and the entity class becomes a sub-class of the form class. For example, if a 'Motor_Cylinder' class is a form of a 'Motor' artifact, a specialization relationship between two classes is added, and the 'Motor' class becomes a sub-class of the 'Motor_Cylinder' class.

Engineers can also define specialization relationships between behaviors, entities, or forms if they wish to represent the same product at different levels of detail [Bock 2009]. Then, a specific 'Motor_A' in a detail design can be a specialization of a 'Motor' concept in a conceptual or preliminary design because all information about physical motors conforming to the former 'Motor_A' also conforms to the latter 'Motor'. In addition, the specialization relationship can save engineers the effort of defining duplicate axioms at the M1 layer. Since specialization implies axiom inheritance, engineers can use specialization relations in order to reuse existing axioms of concepts. For example, if axioms of a 'Motor' artifact exist, a new specialized 'Motor_A' concept inherits the axioms, because all information about physical motors conforming to 'Motor_A' also conforms to the 'Motor' and its axioms. Moreover, the specialization relationship between classes can be inferred by ontological reasoning (i.e., description logic (DL) reasoning). If the axioms of classes at the M1 layer are consistent, ontological reasoning can exploit those axioms to find new specialization relationships between classes. For example, if a designed behavior satisfies a required behavior, entities specified by them should also have a specialization relationship.

5.4 Developing product instances (M1-M0 interactions)

Product models find their realization in the real world as physical items. The interaction between the M1 and M0 layers is necessary to build and trace the relationships between product models and physical items. While the M1 layer represents different views of a product-specific model, the M0 layer represents occurrence or measured information about physical realizations (items) of the model. A physical item at M0 can have multiple behavior occurrences. While designed behaviors at M1 are invariant once they are specified, behavior occurrence information of physical items at M0 is dependent on its observation time and place. Behavior occurrence information may also depend on the accuracy and precision of instruments used, so there can be multiple measurements of the same M0 physical item that gives different values and uncertainties.

The interaction between the M1 and M0 layers is implemented as a conformance relationship.

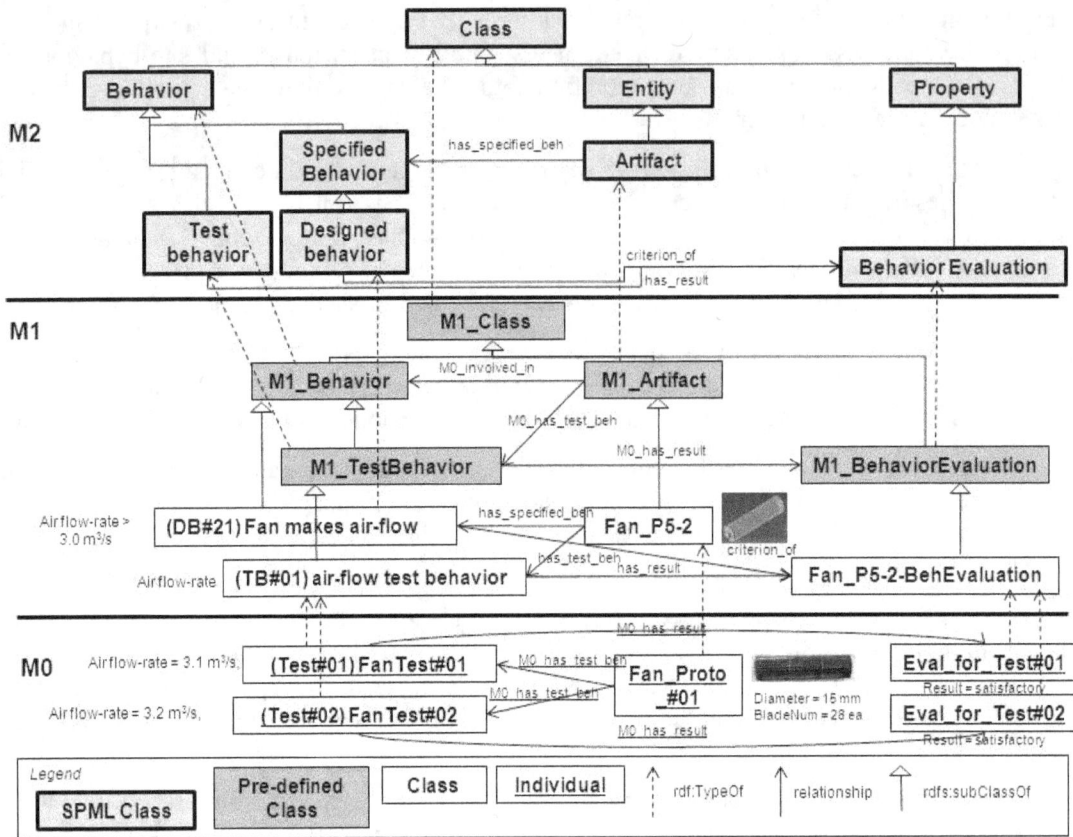

Figure 13. Pre-defined classes at M1 for behavior evaluation of M0 instances.

Conformance relationships between classes at the M1 and instances at the M0 can be established automatically by inference systems if the information pertaining to the instances satisfies the definitions of the classes at the M1 layer. In addition, if the conformance relationship is manually established between a class at the M1 layer and an instance at the M0 layer, the information of the instance should satisfy the definition of the class. For example, let us assume that there is a 'Motor_A' artifact class specialized from a 'MotorCylinder' geometry class whose attribute and value are 'diameter' and '20 mm ± 0.1 mm,' respectively. Every instance of the 'Motor_A' class must have an attribute 'diameter', and its value must be between 19.9 mm and 20.1 mm. These conformances can be checked by ontological inference engines.

A conformance relationship can be also established between a behavior class and behavior occurrence. A behavior occurrence at the M0 layer is used to test (or measure) behavior information of a physical item. A behavior occurrence may or may not satisfy a designed behavior. If a behavior occurrence satisfies a definition of a designed behavior, it means that the physical item performs well as designed. Since engineers learn more from failures than successes, tested behaviors at M0 and their evaluation results should be connected to the respective product model at M1.

SPML has some pre-defined classes at M1 in order to classify M0 instances. 'M1_Artifact,' 'M1_Behavior,' 'M1_TestedBehavior,' and 'M1_BehaviorEvaluation' classes are pre-defined at the M1 layer for behavior conformance. Figure 13 shows the pre-defined classes and their relationships. Every specified behavior class at M1 should be defined as a specialization of the 'M1_Behavior' class, and every test behavior class at M1 should be defined as a specialization of the 'M1_TestedBehavior' class. These specializations allow inference engines to check conformance relationships between a behavior occurrence at M0 and a designed behavior class at

M1. For instance, behavior occurrences (Test#01 and Test#02) in Figure 13 have attributes and whose values satisfy a definition of a designed behavior (DB#21). So, the occurrences can be inferred as instances of the designed behavior, and their behavior evaluations have a result attribute whose value is 'satisfactory.'

While the attribute values of a designed behavior at M1 are given by engineers, the attribute values of a test behavior at M1 cannot be specified until engineers get enough tested behavior occurrence information at M0. So, the test behavior (TB#01) in Figure 13 has an attribute 'Air flow_rate' without its value. However, if an engineer declares that the test behavior has enough occurrences at M0, the attribute may be given a value consistent with the attribute values specified in behavior occurrences at M0, such as '≥ 3.1 m^3/s.'

6. Illustrative case of SPML

In this section, a product design example is provided to illustrate the concepts in the SPML product modeling language. The scenario used in the example is about developing an impeller assembly, which is a sub-assembly of an air-purifier product, and consists of three components such as a fan, motor, and bearing. The air-purifier product is an auto-part installed behind a back-seat of a car under a rear-window, and hence the size of the air-purifier is restricted to the space between the rear-window and shelf behind the back-seat. Figure 14 shows the air-purifier product model and its installation environment. Generally, passengers prefer an air-purifier, which can clean air quickly and quietly. So, the air-purifier should be designed small enough to fit in the given space and move air quickly without much noise. The impeller is a critical sub-assembly of the air-purifier. The air flow-rate of the impeller is determined by the design of its components: fan and motor. A bigger fan can generate more air flow, but the size of the fan is restricted because it should be assembled into the air-purifier with other components. Engineers can make several fan design alternatives under the size restriction by changing material, shape, angle, and numbers of blades in order to satisfy the air flow-rate required for the air-purifier and the noise restriction. Figure 15 shows the impeller model.

Three actors play roles in the scenario. First, a project manager (PM) coordinates the air-purifier design and makes requirements for a fan and motor. Second, a fan designer (FD) makes a fan model to satisfy the requirements given by the PM, including definition of required behaviors for the fan motor. Third, a motor buyer (MB) selects a motor model, from a motor catalog, whose behaviors satisfy the requirements given by a FD and PM.

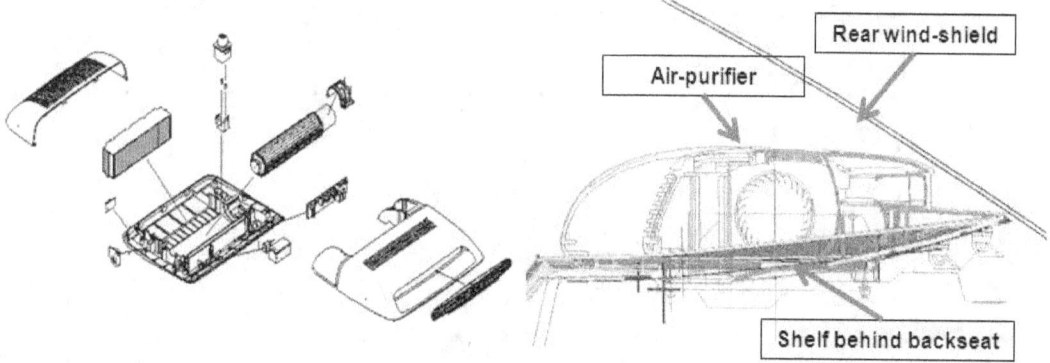

Figure 14. Air-purifier product model and its installation environment.

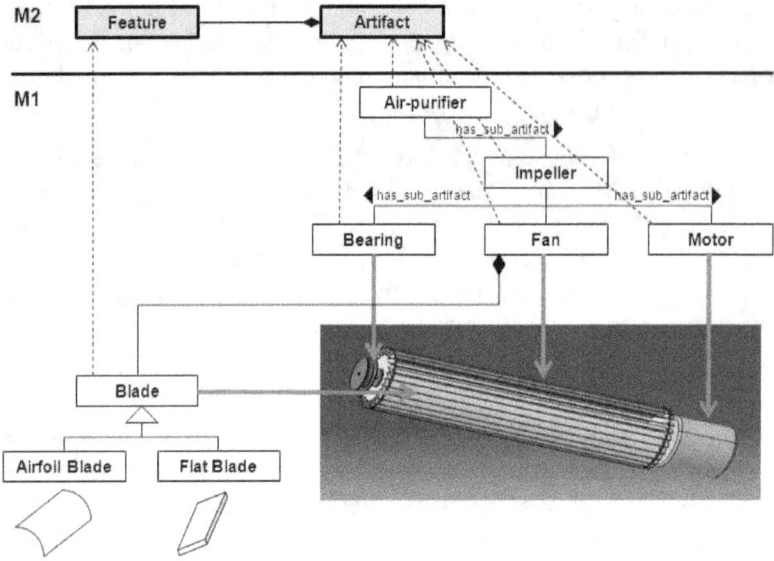

Figure 15. An impeller model and its structure.

The scenario consists of five product design steps: 1) defining requirements of a fan and motor (by PM), 2) making design alternatives of fan (by FD), 3) finding a proper motor model from a market (by MB), 4) after making a design prototype, testing it and evaluating test results (by FD). These steps are performed with the SPML product modeling language and are described below.

1) Defining requirements of a fan and motor (by PM)

Let us assume that a project manager has to develop an air-purifier that should be installed in a car. The PM defines required behaviors of the artifact 'Air-purifier-P5' informally. In Figure 16, the PM defines three informal required behaviors (IB#01), (IB#02), and (IB#03) and one geometry class (G#01) of the artifact. External entities can be also defined from the informal required behaviors.

The PM can define formal required behaviors from the informal required behaviors. The PM can make two formal behaviors like (FB#01) and (FB#02) in Figure 17. Each formal behavior has an attribute and value. The PM can define formal required behaviors of sub-assemblies considering those of the air-purifier. The attribute values are assigned by the PM based on domain expertise.

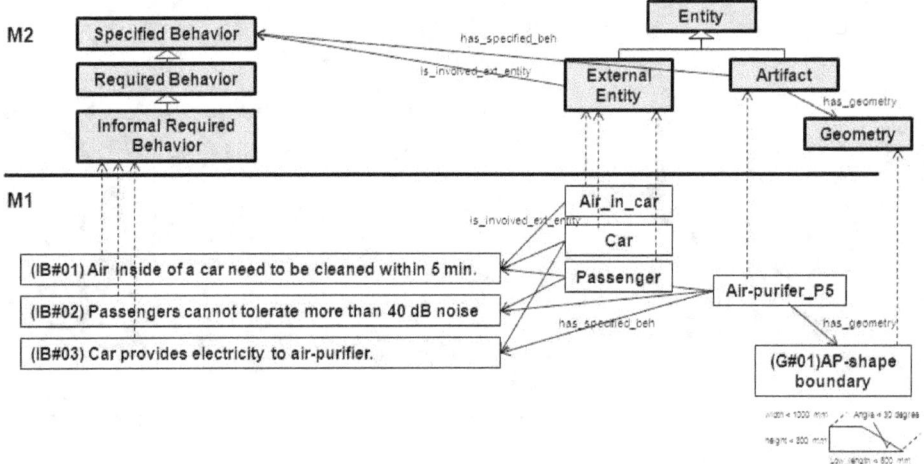

Figure 16. Defining informal required behavior and geometry for an air-purifier.

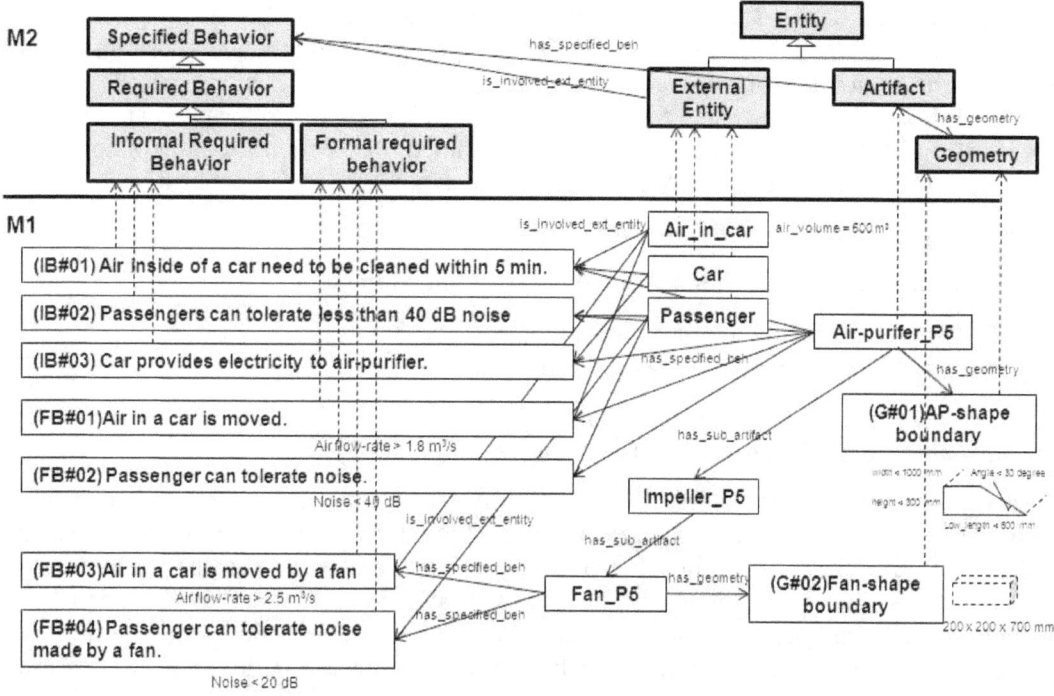

Figure 17. Defining formal required behaviors of a fan.

For example, 'Fan_P5' needs to make more air flow (FB#03) than the air-purifier (FB#01) because the air flow-rate will be reduced after the air flow passes through an air-filter. The PM also makes a component lay-out of the air-purifier, and assigns an available space for a fan. The (G#02) geometry in Figure 17 is a shape boundary of the fan design.

2) Making design alternatives of fan (by FD)

A fan designer (FD) can make many fan design alternatives satisfying the required behavior and forms given by a PM. Design alternatives may have specific design behaviors or forms that

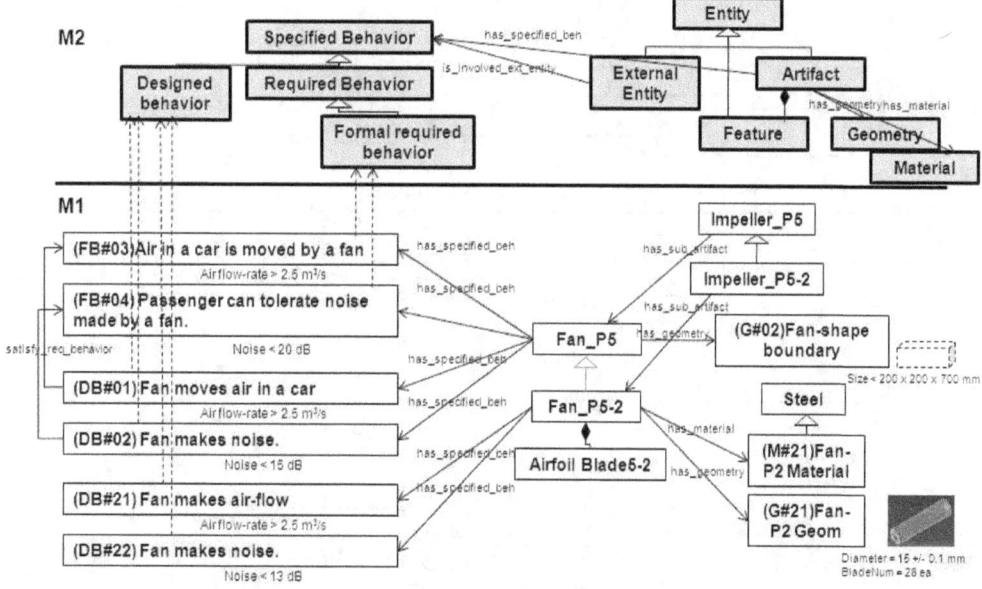

Figure 18. Defining designed behaviors and forms of a fan.

satisfy required behaviors and forms given by a PM. So, each design alternative is defined as a specialization of the 'Fan_P5' as shown in Figure 18. Figure 18 shows the FD's description about 'Fan_P5-2' artifact that has airfoil blades. The 'Fan_P5-2' artifact has more specific designed behaviors and forms than the 'Fan_P5' artifact. So, a specialization relationship can be defined between two artifacts at M1. In addition, as explained in Section 5.3, the relationships 'has_material' and 'has_geometry' at M1 are interpreted as specialization relationships.

3) Selecting a proper motor model (by MB).

Let us assume that two formal required behaviors are defined for a motor design.

- (FB#31) A car provides electricity to a motor.
  attributes: elec_force = 12 V, elec_current = 15 mA.

- (FB#32) Fan_P5-2 is rotated by a motor.
  attributes: rotation_speed > 2000 rpm, torque > 15 Nm.

The formal required behavior (FB#31) can be derived from the informal required behavior (IB#03) in Figure 17. The formal required behavior (FB#31) can be defined by a fan designer after 'Fan_P5-2' is designed. A motor buyer (MB) can define specific designed behaviors that satisfy the required behaviors. Figure 19 shows two designed behaviors (DB#31) and (DB#32) defined by a MB. If designed behaviors of a motor are defined, a definition of the motor can be generated as explained in Section 5.3. The definition of a motor can be used to search a motor design library. Motor models in the design library should also have their definitions with their behaviors including specific attributes. Figure 19 shows an example of inference result of searching a motor design library.

4) Testing a design prototype and evaluating test results (by FD).

After selecting a motor, the FD can make a prototype of the fan design model and tests its behaviors to validate the fan design model. Figure 20 shows an example of testing a fan prototype. The 'Fan_Proto_#01' in the figure is a physical prototype fan, and it has two tested behavior occurrences (Test#01) and (Test#02) that measure air flow-rate and noise level.

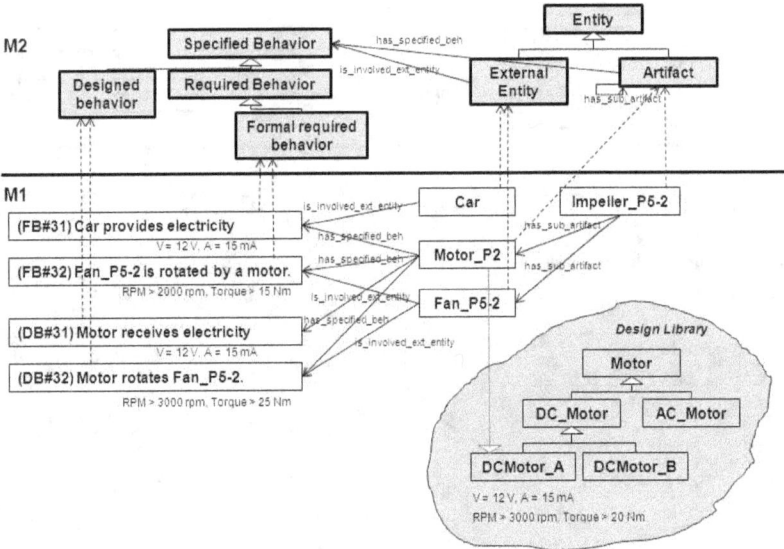

Figure 19. Defining designed behaviors and forms of a fan.

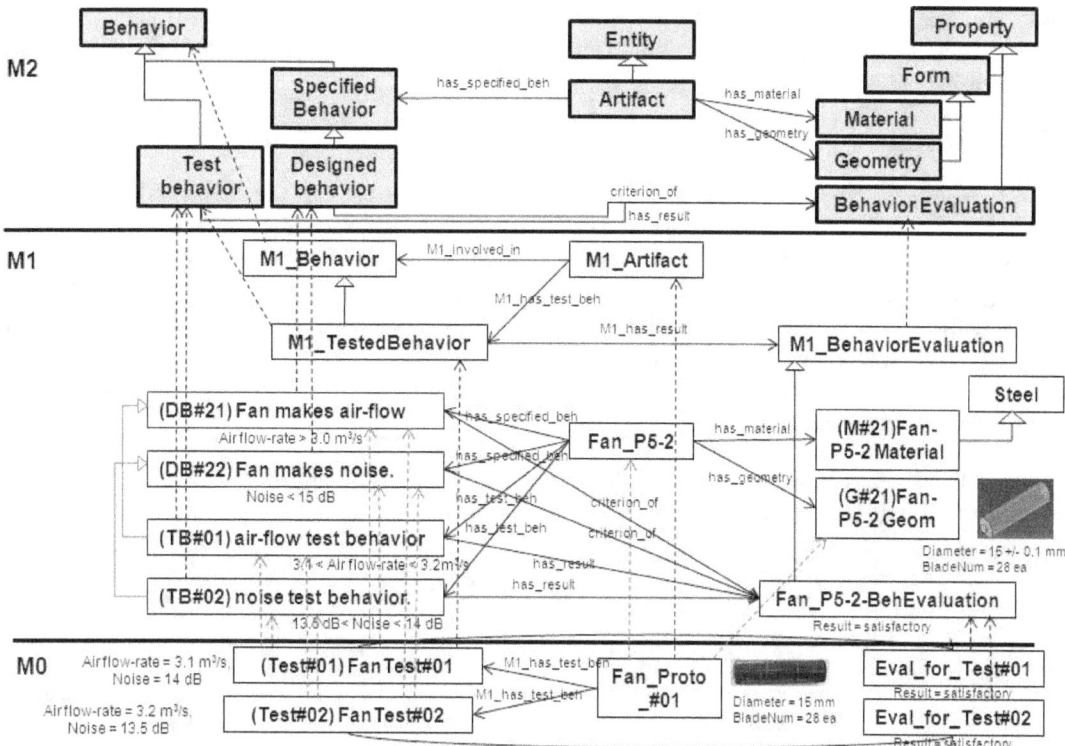

Figure 20. Defining designed behaviors and forms of a fan.

Each tested behavior occurrence can be evaluated, and its evaluation result is recorded. Figure 20 shows the behavior evaluation results of the fan prototype. The 'Fan_Proto_#01' item at M0 can be inferred as an instance of 'Fan_P5-2' model because its form-related attributes and behavior occurrences satisfy the form and designed behaviors of 'Fan_P5-2' artifact at M1.

7. Discussion and Conclusion

In the paper, we extended OWL to SPML to include specific language constructs to define and model product design and manufacturing. The constructs like 'Behavior,' 'Artifact,' etc. are defined in SPML (M2 layer), so that the semantics of these constructs can be exploited by designers and engineers. This will allow designer and engineers to check whether particular entities are behavior, artifact, or other classes in SPML. In OAM, 'Assembly' is a class and not defined in M2 layer. As a next step, the notion of 'Assembly' will be defined in SPML (M2 layer). As mentioned earlier, this will be a powerful feature to check whether an entity is an assembly or not. It is also to be noted that the axioms that define 'Behavior,' 'ExternalEntity,' and 'Artifact' can be extended for specific needs, thus allowing extension to SPML.

The proposed framework needs additional work and implementation in order to be usable as a product modeling system. As mentioned earlier, an SPML editor interface is under development. The editor interface will allow description of product models using methods and terminology familiar to engineers, hiding from them the underlying formal logic-based representation of the product models. In addition, user interfaces for integration with applications such as design knowledge bases and Computer-Aided Design (CAD) systems could be implemented. Then, SPML can be a powerful mechanism for annotating CAD models, so that the CAD models can be semantically enriched with information beyond geometry such as requirement, function, and behavior.

In terms of information modeling scope, SPML currently focuses on product structure and behavior evaluation within a product lifecycle. Additional information modeling issues need to be addressed such as version control, product configuration, assembly relationship, tolerance, and sustainability.

Disclaimer

No approval or endorsement of any commercial product by the National Institute of Standards and Technology is intended or implied. Certain commercial equipments, software, instruments, or materials are identified in this report to facilitate better understanding. Such identification does not imply recommendations or endorsement by the National Institute of Standards and Technology, nor does it imply the materials, software, or equipment identified are necessarily the best available for the purpose.

Acknowledgement

The authors would like to acknowledge the comments and suggestions of Joshua Lubell in improving the report but any residual mistakes remain ours.

References

[Beckett 2004]   D. Beckett and B. McBride. (2004). "RDF/XML syntax specification (Revised) W3C recommendation 10 February 2004." Available: http://www.w3c.org/TR/rdf-syntax-grammar.

[Bock 2009]   C. Bock, X.F. Zha, H.W. Suh, and J.H. Lee (2009). *Ontological product modeling for collaborative design*. NIST interagency/internal report (NISTIR)-7643, National Institute of Standards and Technology (NIST), Gaithersburg, MD, USA.

[Borst 1997]   P. Borst, H. Akkermans, and J. Top (1997). "Engineering ontologies." *International Journal of Human-Computer Studies*, Vol. 46, No. 2-3, pp. 365-406.

[Brachman 2004a] R.J. Brachman and H.J. Levesque (2004a). *Knowledge representation and reasoning*, Elsevier. chapter. 9.

[Brachman 2004b] R.J. Brachman and H.J. Levesque (2004b). *Knowledge representation and reasoning*, Elsevier. chapter. 2.

[Brickley 2004]   D. Brickley, R.V. Guha, and B. McBride. (2004). "RDF vocabulary description language 1.0 : RDF Schema W3C recomendation 10 february 2004." Available: http://www.w3c.org/TR/rdf-schema.

[Chen 1997]   Y.M. Chen and C.L. Wei (1997). "Computer-aided feature-based design for net shape manufacturing." *Computer Integrated Manufacturing Systems*, Vol. 10, No. 2, pp. 147-164.

[Chep 1999]   A. Chep and L. Tricarico (1999). "Object-oriented analysis and design of a manufacturing feature representation." *International Journal of Production Research*, Vol. 37, No. 10, pp. 2349-2376.

[Clark 1999]   J. Clark. (1999). "XSL Transformations (XSLT) Version 1.0 - W3C Recommendation 16 November 1999." Available: http://www.w3.org/TR/xslt.

[Edmond 2007]   C.K. Edmond, X. Chan, and K.M. Yu (2007). "A framework of ontology-enabled product knowledge management." *International Journal of Product Development*, Vol. 4, No. 3-4, pp. 241-254.

[Fenves 2002]   S.J. Fenves (2002). *A core product model for representing design information*. NISTIR-6736, NIST, Gaithersburg.

[Fenves 2005]   S.J. Fenves, S. Foufou, C. Bock, S. Rachuri, N. Bouillon, and R.D. Sriram (2005). *CPM 2: A revised core product model for representing design information*. NIST interagency/internal report (NISTIR)-7185, National Institute of Standards and Technology (NIST), Gaithersburg.

[Genesereth 1992] M.R. Genesereth and R.E. Fikes (1992). *Knowledge interchange format, version 3.0 reference manual*. Technical Report Logic-92-1, Computer Science Department, Stanford University,

[Gorti 1996]   R. Gorti and R.D. Sriram (1996). "From symbol to form: a framework for conceptual design." *Computer-Aided Design*, Vol. 28, No. 11, pp. 853-870.

[Gorti 1998]   S.R. Gorti, A. Gupta, G.J. Kim, R.D. Sriram, and A. Wong (1998). "An object-oriented representation for product and design processes." *Computer-Aided Design*, Vol. 30, No. 7, pp. 489-501.

[Gosling 2005]   J. Gosling, B. Joy, G. Steele, and G. Bracha (2005). *The Java language specification, third edition*, Addison-Wesley.

[Gruber 1995]   T. Gruber (1995). "Toward principles for the design of ontologies used for knowledge sharing." *International Journal Human-Computer Studies*, Vol. 43, No. 5-6, pp. 907-928.

[Gu 1994]   P.H. Gu and Y. Zhang (1994). "OOPPS: an object-oriented process planning system." *Computers & Industrial Engineering*, Vol. 26, No. 4, pp. 709-731.

[Guarino 1997]   N. Guarino, S. Borgo, and C. Masolo (1997). "Logical modelling of product knowledge: towards a well-founded semantics for STEP." *in the Proceedings of the European Conference on Product Data Technology*. pp. 183-190, Sophia Antipolis, France.

[Hirtz 2002]   J. Hirtz, R.B. Stone, D.A. McAdams, S. Szykman, and K.L. Wood (2002). "A functional basis for engineering design: reconciling and evolving previous efforts." *Research in Engineering Design*, Vol. 13, No. pp. 65-82.

[Horridge 2006] M. Horridge, N. Drummond, J. Goodwin, A. rector, R. Stevens, and H.H. Wang (2006). "The Manchester OWL Syntax." *in the Proceedings of the OWL experiences and Directions Workshop (OWLED'06)*.

[Horrocks 2001] I. Horrocks, F.V. Harmelen, P.F. Patel-Schneider, T.B. Lee, D. Brickley, D. Connolly, M. Dean, S. Decker, D. Fensel, R. Fikes, P. Hayes, J. Heflin, J. Hendler, O. Lassila, D. McGuinness, and L.A. Stein. (2001). "DAML+OIL." Available: http://www.daml.org/2001/03/daml+oil-index.html.

[Horrocks 2004] I. Horrocks, P.F. Patel-Schneider, H. Boley, S. Tabet, B. Grosof, and M. Dean. (2004). "SWRL: a semantic web rule language combining OWL and RuleML W3C member submission 21 May 2004." Available: http://www.w3.org/Submission/SWRL/.

[ISO 10303-1 1994] ISO 10303-1 (1994). *Industrial automation systems and integration -- Product data representation and exchange -- Part 1: Overview and fundamental principles*. International Organization for Standardization (ISO), Geneva, Switzerland.

[ISO 10303-11 2004] ISO 10303-11 (2004). *Industrial automation systems and integration -- Product data representation and exchange -- Part 11: Description methods: The EXPRESS language reference manual*. International Organization for Standardization (ISO), Geneva, Switzerland.

[Kim 2006] K.Y. Kim, D.G. Manley, and H. Yang (2006). "Ontology-based assembly design and information sharing for collaborative product development." *Computer-Aided Design*, Vol. 38, No. 12, pp. 1233-1250.

[Kitamura 2002] Y. Kitamura (2002). "A functional concept ontology and its application to automatic identification of functional structures." *Advanced Engineering Informatics*, Vol. 16, No. 2, pp. 145-163.

[Leal 2005] D. Leal (2005). "ISO 15926 Life Cycle Data for Process Plant: an Overview." *Oil and Gas Science and Technology*, Vol. 60, No. 4, pp. 629-638.

[Lee 2008] J. Lee, H. Chae, C.H. Kim, and K. Kim (2008). "Design of product ontology architecture for collaborative enterprises." *Expert Systems with Applications*, Vol. 36, No. 2, pp. 2300-2309.

[Lee 2007] J.H. Lee and H.W. Suh (2007). "OWL-based Product Ontology (POWL) Architecture and Representation for Sharing Product Knowledge on a Web." *in the Proceedings of the ASME 2007 International Design Engineering Technical Conferences Computers and Information in Engineering Conference (IDETC/CIE)*, Las Vegas, NV, USA.

[Lee 2009] J.H. Lee and H.W. Suh (2009). "Ontology-based multi-layered knowledge framework for product lifecycle management." *Concurrent Engineering Researches and Applications*, Vol. 16, No. 4, pp. 301-311.

[Liang 2008] V.C. Liang, C. Bock, and X.F. Zha (2008). *An ontological modeling platform*. NIST interagency/internal report (NISTIR)-7509, National Institute of Standards and Technology (NIST), Gaithersburg, MD, USA.

[Lin 1996] J.X. Lin, M.S. Fox, and T. Bilgic (1996). "A requirement ontology for engineering design." *Concurrent Engineering Research and Applications*, Vol. 4, No. 3, pp. 279-291.

[McGuinness 2004] D.L. McGuinness and F.V. Harmelen. (2004). "OWL web ontology language overview W3C Recommendation 10 February 2004." Available: http://www.w3.org/TR/owl-features/.

[Niles 2001] I. Niles and A. Pease (2001). "Towards a Standard Upper Ontology." *in the Proceedings of the 2nd International Conference on Formal Ontology in Information Systems (FOIS-2001)*, Ogunquit, Maine.

[OMG 2001] OMG. (2001). "Unified modeling language specification v1.4." Available: http://www.omg.org/cgi-bin/doc?formal/01-09-67.

[OMG 2003] OMG. (2003). "Meta object facility (MOF) core specification, OMG available specification, version 2.0." Available: http://www.omg.org/spec/MOF/2.0/PDF.

[OMG 2007] OMG. (2007). "Model-Driven Architecture." Available: http://www.omg.org/mda.

[Patil 2005]   L. Patil, D. Dutta, and R.D. Sriram (2005). "Ontology-based exchange of product data semantics." *IEEE Transactions on Automation Science and Engineering*, Vol. 2, No. 3, pp. 213-255.

[Rachuri 2006]   S. Rachuri, Y. Han, S. Foufou, S. Feng, U. Roy, Fujun W., R.D. Sriram, and K. Lyons (2006). "A model for capturing product assembly information." *Journal of Computing and Information Science in Engineering*, Vol. 6, No. 1, pp. 11-21.

[Srinivasan 2009] V. Srinivasan (2009). "An integration framework for product lifecycle management." *Computer-Aided Design*, doi:10.1016/j.cad.2008.12.001.

[Sriram 2002]   R.D. Sriram and S. Szykman (2002). *The NIST design repository project: project overview and implementation design*. NIST interagency/internal report (NISTIR)-6926, National Institute of Standards and Technology (NIST), Gaithersburg, MD, USA.

[Stokes 2001]   M. Stokes (2001). *Managing engineering knowledge: MOKA methodology for knowledge based engineering applications*, Professional Engineering Publishing.

[Szykman 2001a] S. Szykman, S.J. Fenves, W. Keirouz, and S.B. Shooter (2001a). "A foundation for interoperability in next-generation product development systems." *Computer-Aided Design*, Vol. 33, No. 7, pp. 549-559.

[Szykman 2001b] S. Szykman, R.D. Sriram, and W. Regli (2001b). "The role of knowledge in next-generation product development systems." *Journal of Computing and Information Science in Engineering*, Vol. 1, No. 3, pp. 3-11.

[Weissman 2009] A. Weissman, S.K. Gupta, X. Fiorentini, S. Rachuri, and R.D. Sriram (2009). *Formal representation of product design specifications for validating product designs*. NIST interagency/internal report (NISTIR)-7626, National Institute of Standards and Technology (NIST), Gaithersburg, MD, USA.

[Yang 2008]   D. Yang, M. Dong, and R. Miao (2008). "Development of a product configuration system with an ontology-based approach." *Computer-Aided Design*, Vol. 40, No. 8, pp. 863-878.

www.ingramcontent.com/pod-product-compliance
Lightning Source LLC
Chambersburg PA
CBHW080357290526
45791CB00009BA/2903